# STEM IN

# BASKETBALL

SportsZone

Imprint of Abdo Publishing
abdopublishing.com

JESSAMINE COUNTY PUBLIC LIBRARY
600 South Main Street
Nicholasville, KY 40356

BY ANGIE SMIBERT

ABDOPUBLISHING.COM

Published by Abdo Publishing, a division of ABDO, PO Box 398166, Minneapolis, Minnesota 55439.
Copyright © 2018 by Abdo Consulting Group, Inc. International copyrights reserved in all countries.
No part of this book may be reproduced in any form without written permission from the
publisher. SportsZone™ is a trademark and logo of Abdo Publishing.

Printed in the United States of America, North Mankato, Minnesota
102017
012018

THIS BOOK CONTAINS
RECYCLED MATERIALS

Cover Photo: Jeff Chiu/AP Images
Interior Photos: Jeff Chiu/AP Images, 1; Monkey Business Images/Shutterstock Images, 4–5, 45;
Bettmann/Getty Images, 7; Jim Mone/AP Images, 9; Lenny Ignelzi/AP Images, 11; Austin Mcafee/Cal
Sport Media/AP Images, 12–13; Shutterstock Images, 15, 20–21; John Raoux/AP Images, 17; Ethan
Miller/Getty Images News/Getty Images, 23; Garik Prost/Shutterstock Images, 25 (court); Cherdchai
Charasri/Shutterstock Images, 25 (ball), 38; Rodrigo Reyes Marin/AFLO/Newscom, 27; AP Images,
28–29; Eric Gay/AP Images, 30; Paul Beaty/AP Images, 33; Brian Kersey/AP Images, 35; Stacy Bengs/
AP Images, 36–37; Red Line Editorial, 38; David Zalubowski/AP Images, 40; Mark Von Holden/AP for
Dove® Men+Care®/AP Images, 42–43

Editor: Arnold Ringstad
Series Designer: Maggie Villaume
Content Consultant: Misti R. Wajciechowski, M.Ed., Assistant Professor, Teaching and Learning,
    Virginia Commonwealth University

PUBLISHER'S CATALOGING-IN-PUBLICATION DATA

Names: Smibert, Angie, author.
Title:  STEM in basketball / by Angie Smibert.
Description: Minneapolis, Minnesota : Abdo Publishing, 2018. | Series: STEM in sports | Includes
    online resources and index.
Identifiers: LCCN 2017946881 | ISBN 9781532113482 (lib.bdg.) | ISBN 9781532152368 (ebook)
Subjects: LCSH:  Basketball--Juvenile literature. | Sports sciences--Juvenile literature. | Physics--
    Juvenile literature.
Classification: DDC 796.323--dc23
LC record available at https://lccn.loc.gov/2017946881

TABLE OF CONTENTS

From youth basketball to the professional level, STEM principles are always in play.

# NOTHING BUT NET!

**T**he team is down by two points. Only three seconds are left in the game. Isabelle snatches the rebound. She has a split-second decision to make: dribble or pass? She knows it would take her at least four seconds to run down the court at full speed. She sees Kelsey on the move. Isabelle hurls the ball. Two seconds later, it meets Kelsey at the perfect spot for a three-pointer. Kelsey plants her feet, bends her knees, and leaps eight inches (20 cm) in the air. She releases the ball at a 55-degree angle, with two revolutions per second of backspin. The ball soars in an arc toward the basket. The angle drops the ball into the net. *Swish!* The buzzer sounds, and the team rushes out onto the court to celebrate!

Of course, Isabelle and Kelsey weren't thinking about all the angles, vectors, numbers, and forces in those three seconds. But these concepts in science, technology, engineering, and math (STEM) are visible in every game of basketball.

## HISTORY OF BASKETBALL

Basketball's inventor wasn't thinking about the science, either. He was thinking about giving his students a sport to play in the winter. In December 1891, Dr. James Naismith took over a physical education class at a school in Springfield, Massachusetts. Many of the students already played football and rugby. They weren't satisfied with playing traditional indoor games. The new sport needed to be simple to learn, yet challenging to play. Naismith borrowed ideas from a few other sports.

**Basketball has changed a great deal since Naismith's day.**

He came up with 13 rules for the new game. Naismith hung up peach baskets in the school's gymnasium. With these first baskets, the sport of basketball was born.

In modern basketball, each team has five players on the court. They can move the ball by passing or dribbling. Tackling and rough contact aren't allowed. The goal is to get the ball in the opposing side's basket. When a ball goes in, a team gets points. The team with the most points wins the game.

When Naismith's students graduated, they took the sport home with them. Today, basketball is popular worldwide. The International Federation of Basketball Associations (FIBA) is the organization that oversees the sport. It includes basketball associations from 213 countries. Men, women, girls, and boys play in leagues in those countries. The world's premier men's league is the National Basketball Association (NBA). The top women's league is the Women's National Basketball Association (WNBA). Both are based in the United States.

WNBA star Nneka Ogwumike was named the league's most valuable player in 2016.

## STEM ON THE COURTS

STEM concepts are always in play on the basketball court. Science is behind the way both the player and the ball move. When a player bends her knees and jumps, she exerts force against the floor to propel her upward.

She shoots the ball, and several forces work against it as it arcs toward the basket.

Teams use technology to analyze and improve their players' games. Wearable sensors track movement and vital signs. Sensors in the ball can collect statistics. Camera-based player tracking systems capture everything on the court. Researchers have even used computer simulations to come up with the ideal way to shoot a free throw.

Engineering has solved several problems on the court. Backboards once shattered when players slam dunked with too much force. Breakaway rims eliminated this. Timekeepers once had trouble stopping the clock at the instant a referee blew a whistle. Now, digital whistle systems stop the clock automatically when the whistle is blown. And uniforms can be made from recycled plastic while keeping players cool and dry.

Math is also at work whenever a player passes the ball or eyes the angle to the basket. If she's moving,

Each time NBA star Steph Curry makes a three-point shot, he must be sure to release the ball at the correct speed and angle.

the player must think about her own movement as well as her teammate's to figure out where to pass the ball. On a shot, the ball has to approach the basket at the right angle to go in the hoop. STEM is important off the court, too. Teams manage their players using statistics, and fans crunch numbers when filling in predictions for tournament brackets. From the locker room to warm-ups to championship games, STEM plays a key role in basketball.

Memphis Grizzlies player Wayne Selden Jr. dunks the ball during the 2017 NBA Playoffs.

# 2

# THE SCIENCE OF MOTION

One of the most thrilling shots in basketball is a slam dunk. Players leap high into the air, then throw the ball downward through the hoop. A slam dunk is physics in motion. Players almost seem to hover in the air before stuffing the ball in the basket. This illusion is known as hang time. What causes it?

When a player jumps for a dunk, he launches himself high into the air using nearly all the muscles in his legs. However, gravity is constantly pulling him downward. His vertical speed decreases until it reaches zero. At this moment, he is at the top of his jump. Then he begins falling. Because his speed is lower at the top of the jump, he spends more time there. In a slam dunk, about 71 percent of the total jump time is spent in the top half of the jump. Only 29 percent is spent in the bottom, faster half. This creates the illusion of hanging in the air.

## JUMP SHOTS

In one smooth motion, a player bends her knees, raises the ball, jumps, and shoots. The ball arcs toward the basket. This is known as a jump shot. It was not commonly used in professional games until the 1940s. Before that, players often stood still while shooting. One early player who used the jump shot scored 63 points in a 1949 game. Now the jump shot is an essential basketball skill.

Why do jump shots work better? There are many reasons. For one thing, a jump shot raises the ball above

**TOP HALF OF JUMP:**
71% OF TIME

**BOTTOM HALF OF JUMP:**
29% OF TIME

During a slam dunk, a player appears to hang in the air. Gravity slows the player's momentum and pulls him downward. However, moving his arm (and the ball) in the top part of the jump can add to the illusion. When he slams the ball downward, his body rises.

the defenders' heads. This gives the shooter a clearer look at the basket. But perhaps the biggest advantage is that a player can release the ball closer to the basket. From this height, the ball is thrown in a high arc, sailing through the air. The shape of this arc means that the ball can fall downward through the basket at a high angle. This creates a bigger target that is easier for players to hit.

## MUSCLE MEMORY

The first time someone shoots a free throw, she is probably not that good at it. The more she practices, though, the better she gets at the skill. At first this is a slow process, but one day the shot becomes natural. She doesn't really have to think about it as she shoots.

By practicing, the player is using muscle memory. The memory isn't really made in the muscles. It's stored in the brain. The skill enters the long-term memory in a part of the brain called the cerebellum. This part of the brain controls movements.

Practicing free throws helps to sharpen a player's muscle memory.

The first few times the player shoots a free throw, her brain is encoding the memory. It is recording what the movement is. Once the memory is stored in the cerebellum, it can be more quickly recalled. Experts don't agree on how many repetitions it takes to perfect a skill.

## FORCES ACTING ON THE BALL

When a player passes or shoots the ball, she exerts a force on the ball. But her force is not the only one in play. A basketball flying through the air has four forces acting on it: gravity, buoyancy, drag, and the Magnus effect. Gravity is the dominant force, but the other three affect the movement of the ball, too.

Gravity is the force that pulls something toward the center of a massive object. In the case of objects on Earth, it pulls things down to the planet's surface.

### THE FORCE IS IN THE KNEES

The power in the jump shot comes from bending the knees. When a player bends her knees, she is able to use the force of straightening her knees to generate more power and add more force to the shot. When she pushes against the floor, the floor pushes back, sending her upward into a jump.

The basketball is pulled downward as soon as it leaves the player's hand, and the upward movement of the shot begins to slow.

Buoyancy is the upward force that a fluid exerts on an object. In scientific terms, a fluid can be a liquid or a gas. The atmosphere is a fluid, so it exerts a small upward force on the ball.

Drag is created when a solid object pushes against a fluid. The fluid pushes back, slowing the object. As the basketball moves through the air, the air slows it down.

The Magnus effect acts when the ball is spinning. When it spins, the drag force hits the ball unevenly. The ball pushes the air one way, and the air pushes back in the opposite direction. This is the Magnus effect. It curves the path of the ball through the air. The effect is small but noticeable.

Studying angles and rotation can help players develop the perfect free throw.

# 3

# HIGH-TECH PLAY

**T**wo researchers at North Carolina State University used computer simulations to analyze free throws. From these simulations, the researchers developed a formula for a successful free throw. First, players should shoot so that the ball has three revolutions per second of backspin as it flies through the air. Second, they should launch the ball at an angle of 52 degrees. Third, they should aim at a spot 2.8 inches (7.1 cm) back from the center of the hoop. Finally, they should release the ball as high as possible.

According to the researchers, all of these factors make the ball more likely to go in the basket. Backspin causes the ball to soften its bounce when it hits the rim or backboard. Releasing the ball as high as possible and at that particular angle creates an arc that delivers the ball into the basket.

## WEARABLE TECHNOLOGY

Just like other athletes, basketball players are using wearable technology to improve their games and fitness. Common pieces of wearable tech, such as fitness tracker

## SMART BASKETBALLS

Several companies have designed basketballs with built-in sensors. These smart basketballs can track baskets, rebounds, and other statistics. The balls' sensors connect with smartphone apps. Some apps allow players to compete against other people around the world. Others give the player a chance to focus on improving certain skills, such as free throws.

JUMPS

76

Session Time: 1642.4 [secs]

A wearable device tracks the number of times a person jumps.

bracelets, have built in sensors that measure steps and heart rate. However, the wearable tech that players are using does much more. Some devices made especially for basketball measure acceleration, the vertical height of jumps, and even hang time. Players can use these in practice or training to focus on areas they want to improve.

Wrist trackers, however, don't always give precise or accurate enough data. Many companies are already working on clothing and shoes with built-in sensors. These might be the future of wearable tech in sports.

## PLAYER TRACKING SYSTEMS

In the 2017–18 season, the NBA began using a camera-based player tracking system during all games. The new technology records a complete game for analysis. Optical trackers capture every move of the ball and the players. These trackers record positions 25 times a second. This creates a huge amount of new data to study.

The company Stats LLC offers its tracking technology to NBA teams. In this system, six cameras are placed in the rafters of the arena. The cameras track the location of all the players, identifying them based on jersey numbers. They also track the ball's position. Using all this data, teams can view exact replays of all the movement on the court during a game. Different teams are finding different ways to use the data they collect. The tracking system costs teams about $100,000 per year.

Using the system, teams can analyze everything from the position of an individual player's body to the success rates of certain shots. Coaches and players can use the information to adapt strategy and training.

## VIRTUAL REALITY

Some professional basketball leagues have begun to use virtual reality (VR) for their fans. VR is a computer-generated simulation of a three-dimensional world. VR lets the user look around a virtual space as if he or she were there. In 2017 the NBA offered fans the option to experience its All-Star Game in virtual reality. On the court, 360-degree cameras captured the action. The fans wore popular VR headsets to watch the game from anywhere in the world.

In 2017 the NBA announced another use for VR. It will be used to help train referees. Wearing VR headsets, referees will be able to practice in a virtual world before they set foot on an actual court.

Virtual reality technology can help fans connect with the game.

Engineers have helped solve the issue of shattering glass backboards.

# 4

# ENGINEERING GAME CHANGERS

**A** player slams the ball into the hoop. He grabs the rim and pulls down hard. The backboard shatters, and glass rains down on the court. For decades in the NBA and NCAA, backboards shattered. Players got hurt, and games were delayed—and even cancelled. Breakaway rims changed all that. Thanks to some clever engineering, this type of accident no longer happens.

TORQUE

DOWNWARD
FORCE

During the 2016 Olympics, DeAndre Jordan pulls on the rim after a slam dunk. He's creating torque, a twisting force. The springs in the breakaway rim absorb the force. They prevent the backboard from shattering.

In the older design, the rim was bolted to a metal plate sandwiched between sheets of glass. When a player pulled on the rim, it resulted in a twisting force called torque. It made the plate flex forward, shattering the glass. To create enough torque to shatter the glass, the player had to apply a lot of force and grab the rim at the farthest point from the glass.

To fix this problem, engineers redesigned the rim and backboard. Now, the rim is attached to the post, and it is on springs. When a player pulls a rim downward, the springs absorb the torque. The rim bends, then snaps back into place after the player lets go.

## SHATTERING BACKBOARDS

Not every player can shatter an old-school glass backboard. A player needs to be able to generate at least 250 pounds of force to pull the rim down—and another 625 pounds to shatter the glass. A player's force equals his mass times acceleration ($F=ma$). In other words, a big player can easily generate enough force to shatter the glass. Some players can hit the rim with more than 1,000 pounds of force.

## DIGITAL WHISTLES

During a game, every time the referee blows his whistle, the game clock has to stop. Until recently, a timekeeper operated the clock. He or she listened for the referee's whistle and stopped the clock. This left room for human error. During the course of a whole game, it could waste several seconds.

To solve this problem, the NBA installed a new timing system that responds to a whistle. When a referee's whistle blows, the system stops the clock automatically. A tiny microphone picks up the signal and relays it to a small box clipped to the referee's belt. The box wirelessly transmits the signal to the timing system, and the clock stops. To restart the clock, the referee presses a button on the box.

## RECYCLED UNIFORMS

For the 2016 Summer Olympics, the US national basketball team wore uniforms made from

US player Carmelo Anthony wore a recycled uniform in the 2016 Summer Olympics.

recycled plastic. The uniforms were also designed to reduce sweat. To make this type of fabric, the manufacturer chops up plastic bottles. The tiny pieces are melted into thread, which is then spun into yarn. The result is lighter, more breathable fabric.

Uniform makers also used technology to design the uniforms themselves. They mapped the players' sweat using sensors. This told designers exactly where the players sweat most. The new uniform was designed to be lighter and more vented in these areas.

## BALL REDESIGN

Not every engineering design is successful. For the 2006–07 season, the NBA introduced a new ball. It was the first time the league had changed the ball in 35 years. The old ball was made from leather and had eight panels. The new ball was made from synthetic materials. The panels were sewn together in an interlocking cross pattern. The new design improved grip and eliminated the need for a break-in period.

The new synthetic ball became unpopular with players soon after its introduction.

However, the players hated it. Their chief complaint was that the ball caused cuts and abrasions on their hands. The NBA players' union even filed a grievance against the league. The NBA quickly went back to the old leather ball. It is still using the old ball today.

Tulsa Shock player Temeka Johnson passes the ball around an opponent in a 2012 game.

# 5

# A GAME OF NUMBERS

**W**henever a player passes a ball or takes a shot while moving, she has to take into account her own speed and direction to get the ball in the right spot. If the teammate is moving, the player needs to take the teammate's speed and direction into account, too. Without really thinking about it, she's adding vectors.

A vector is a way of showing something's movement, including both direction and speed. It is represented with

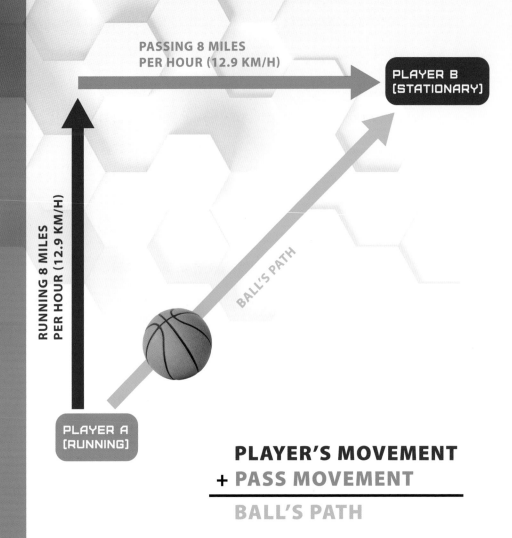

**PASSING 8 MILES
PER HOUR (12.9 KM/H)**

**PLAYER B
[STATIONARY]**

**RUNNING 8 MILES
PER HOUR (12.9 KM/H)**

**BALL'S PATH**

**PLAYER A
[RUNNING]**

# PLAYER'S MOVEMENT
## + PASS MOVEMENT
## BALL'S PATH

Players calculate vectors every time they pass the ball.
Player A needs to pass the ball to player B. Both have a
speed and a direction. To add vectors, simply put the arrow
for the player's motion and the arrow for the pass's motion
head to tail. It doesn't matter what order they're in. Then
draw a third arrow going from the tail of one arrow to the
head of the other. The result points to where the ball will go.

an arrow pointed in the direction of the motion. The length of the arrow indicates the speed. Vectors can be used to illustrate how a player's own motion is combined with the motion she gives the ball when she passes it.

## ADVANCED STATS AND PACE

Basketball teams have always kept statistics on players and teams. Traditional stats include points, rebounds, assists, steals, blocks, and shooting percentages. For instance, a player's shooting percentage equals the number of shots made divided by the number attempted. If a player makes 75 shots out of 100 attempted, his shooting percentage is 75 percent. Stats help players and teams analyze and improve their games.

But these numbers don't always give coaches the whole picture. Some teams play a faster game than others. So the NBA and WNBA use advanced statistics. These stats account for the differences in pace. Mathematically, pace is the number of possessions, or

Portland Trail Blazers coach Nate McMillan examines a sheet of
statistics during a 2010 game.

times that a team has the ball, per game. Faster teams

have the ball more often in a game than teams that

prefer a slower pace. So comparing stats per game

doesn't give the coaches a true picture of one team

versus another. Advanced stats are based on 100

possessions, rather than one game. Comparing points or shooting percentages per 100 possessions gives coaches and players a truer average picture of their performance based on how often the team gets the ball.

## THE PERFECT BRACKET

In March of every year, 68 teams from men's college basketball's largest division play in a tournament known as March Madness. This tournament determines the national champion. Four teams are eliminated before the first official round, leaving 64 teams. Before the tournament starts, fans like to fill out a bracket. This is a chart with all of the games on it. Fans predict which team is going to win each game. A perfect bracket is one where all of the winners are picked correctly. What chance does someone have to fill out a perfect bracket?

Let's start with a much smaller tournament. If four teams are in the tournament, that means three games will be played. When filling out the bracket randomly, there are two possible ways to fill out each game.

With three games and two possible outcomes for each,
the number of outcomes can be found by multiplying
2 times 2 times 2. This can also be written as 2 to the
power of 3, or $2^3$. The result is 8. Only one of these

Fans across the country enjoy filling out March Madness brackets.

8 possible outcomes for the tournament is correct, so there is a 1-in-8 chance of filling out a perfect bracket.

In a 64-team bracket, there are 63 games total. The probability of filling out a perfect bracket is then $2^{63}$.

This is an incredibly huge number: about 9 quintillion, or 9 followed by 18 zeroes. So a fan has a 1 in 9 quintillion chance of randomly filling out a perfect bracket.

However, the real odds aren't quite so simple. Fans do not pick winning teams randomly. If they know a lot about basketball, they may be better at choosing the likely winners. A knowledgeable fan might be able to whittle those odds down to 1 in 128 billion. However, no known perfect bracket has ever been filled out.

## FUTURE OF STEM IN BASKETBALL

On and off the court, STEM will continue to be a major factor in basketball. It's always been a game of motion and numbers. Technology and engineering are

MATH IN ACTION

### GEOMETRY OF A BANK SHOT

A player banks the ball off the backboard. Swish! It flies cleanly into the basket. This type of shot is all about the angles. The angle at which the ball hits the backboard is called the angle of incidence. The angle at which the ball bounces is called the angle of reflection. If there's no spin on the ball, the two angles are equal.

Players at all levels can use STEM to improve their game.

relatively new to the sport, but they'll be playing bigger and bigger roles in the future. Coaches, trainers, and players will use cutting-edge technology to improve performance and the fan experience. The next time the ball arcs toward the basket, a player slams the rim, or a referee blows a whistle, be sure to consider the STEM disciplines that are at play.

# GLOSSARY

## BUOYANCY
The ability of an object to float in water or air.

## CEREBELLUM
The back part of the brain that controls balance and the use of muscles.

## FLUID
A substance that moves and flows easily, such as water or air.

## PROBABILITY
The chance that something will happen.

## SENSOR
A device that detects something, such as motion, heat, light, or sound.

## SIMULATION
Something that is made to look, feel, or behave like something else, especially so that it can be studied or used to train people.

## STATISTIC
A number that represents a piece of information.

## SYNTHETIC
Produced artificially.

## TORQUE
A force that causes something to rotate.

## VECTOR
A quantity that has an amount and a direction.

## VIRTUAL REALITY
An artificial world of images and sounds created by a computer.

# ● ONLINE RESOURCES

**Booklinks**
**NONFICTION NETWORK**
FREE! ONLINE NONFICTION RESOURCES

To learn more about STEM in basketball, visit
**abdobooklinks.com**. These links are routinely monitored and
updated to provide the most current information available.

# ● MORE INFORMATION

## BOOKS

Graves, Will. *Make Me the Best Basketball Player*. Minneapolis,
MN: Abdo Publishing, 2017.

Silverman, Drew. *Basketball*. Minneapolis, MN: Abdo
Publishing, 2012.

Williams, Doug. *Great Moments in Olympic Basketball*.
Minneapolis, MN: Abdo Publishing, 2015.

# INDEX

# ABOUT THE AUTHOR

Angie Smibert is the author of several young adult and middle grade novels, numerous short stories, and dozens of educational titles just like this one. She was a science writer for NASA, the US Department of Energy, and the US Environmental Protection Agency.